101 of the
Dumbest Things
People Have Done

Comfort . . . for those who do dumb things

Bridge-Logos

Alachua, Florida 32615

101 of the Dumbest Things People Have Done

Published by:
Bridge-Logos
Alachua, Florida 32615, USA
www.bridgelogos.com

Cartoons by Richard Gunther

Cover illustration by Erik Hollander

Edited by Lynn Copeland

Cover, page design, and production by Genesis Group (www.genesis-group.net)

Cover photo by Carol Scott, Covina, CA (www.cj-studio.com)

Library of Congress Control Number: 2008927772

ISBN 978-0-88270-555-2

Printed in the United States of America

To the two kind people who,
after reading this book,
sent sympathy cards to my wife

Foreword

Ray Comfort should have been born with a warning label on his forehead: "KEEP AWAY; HAZARDOUS TO YOUR HEALTH." My world was a safe one until I met him, and I've never known a dull moment since.

When Ray's around, there is always some mess to clean up, some broken bone to mend, some gaping wound to bandage, some worldwide catastrophe to avert. If there is a button that says "DO NOT PRESS," he is sure to press it; if something is labeled "INDESTRUCTIBLE," he will somehow manage to destroy it; if anyone is within 10 miles of him (wearing full-body armor), they are sure to sustain serious bodily injury.

So if you see a fast-moving, 5'5", 150 pound, mustached Kiwi on the loose... KEEP AWAY! Ray Comfort is dangerous to your health! In fact, Ray is so dangerous, he inspired me (years ago) to write a song that contained the following line:

> When everything is breaking,
> and everyone's left aching,
> then there is no mistaking:
> Ray Comfort's in town!

Of this one thing I am sure: the day will come when Ray Comfort will somehow, in some way, set off a chain of events that will lead to the destruction of the entire universe. When this happens, remember: you heard it first from me.

EMEAL ("E.Z.") ZWAYNE

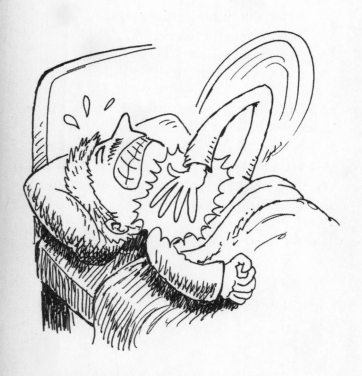

1. *The Mosquito*

Life has been anything but boring since I started getting "floaters." Floaters are little specks that actually float in or on the eyeball. I was told by my eye doctor that they are very common, and can disappear as quickly as they appear.

It was a Monday night, and I woke up around midnight and got out of bed to read. I have been getting up most nights each week for about twenty-five years. Earlier that night my daughter, Rachel, had been telling her kids about how I had perfected walking in the dark. If I couldn't see, I would extend my crossed arms to keep me from walking into any open doors. Pretty clever.

I didn't need to cross my arms this night because I was going into the sunroom. I carefully shut the door making sure not to wake my wife, Sue, who was soundly sleeping upstairs. After thirty minutes I stood up, turned the light off, and in the now pitch dark *walked straight into the closed door!* The bang was so loud I thought for sure that I had awakened Sue.

In the morning I was surprised to find that she didn't hear the big bang. I guess she is used to hearing stumbling noises in the night. She did, however, notice the blood on the bridge of my nose. We were both amazed at how hard I would have had to hit the door to flatten my nose and get a wound on the bridge between my eyes.

That night I trimmed my fingernails, not bothering to file them after trimming (that's a "woman" thing), and then leaped into bed. However, somehow between the bathroom and the bed I managed to cut my left thumb with a sharp nail and draw blood. Sue wasn't surprised.

The next day I fell off my bike, and only slightly injured my left knee. My consolation was that it wasn't as bad as when I rode into a five-inch-high edge of the sidewalk and went over the handlebars.

After sending half a cup of tea down my windpipe and nearly drowning myself during the evening, I jumped into bed that night and began reading a good book, thrilled that I had made it through another day without injuring myself too badly. Suddenly I was distracted by a huge mosquito that flitted between my face and the book. It was one of those blood-filled ones, and because it was so heavy laden and therefore slow, I knew I could kill it.

With the reflexes and agility of a world champion Kung Fu expert, I slapped my open hand against my chest at lightning speed, trapping that beast with such force that it not only startled Sue, but it *really* hurt my bare chest. But it was worth the pain. I focused my eyes on my stinging chest as I searched for its crushed body. I never found it. It was a "floater."

2. *Went Over With a Bang*

Two men in their twenties met with a group of singles for a Fourth of July celebration. Of course, they wanted to impress the young ladies. And they did. They filled a plastic container with dry ice, and made a dry ice bomb. When it exploded with a loud bang, it really impressed the girls. The explosion also impressed the neighbors. They called the police who arrested the pair for making an explosive device. They were jailed for the weekend at $500,000 bail.

3. *Save the Whales*

In Oregon, some clever state Highway Division authorities decided that they would use dynamite to blow up a dead beached whale, rather than go to the trouble and expense of burying the rotting 8-ton mammal. They surmised that after it was blown up, the hundreds of hungry seagulls that were hanging around would then eat the bite-sized portions of the big creature, and the problem would be solved. The crowds and news media were moved back a quarter of a mile and the dynamite was exploded.

Unfortunately, thousands of pieces of rotten whale flesh landed on the crowd, with one 3-foot by 5-foot whale portion landing on a spectator's car, caving the roof in about 18 inches. The noise of the explosion caused the birds to completely disappear, leaving authorities with the exciting job of picking up the thousands of pieces of stinking whale and burying them.

4.

Perfection

I was in Southern California waiting to speak at a Sunday night meeting, when I decided to go to the restroom to make sure I looked presentable. I checked in the mirror to see if my tie was straight. It was perfect. I also had a matching handkerchief in the top pocket of my jacket and a gold pin holding down the knot part of the tie. It was hard to leave the mirror, but I pulled myself away.

As I was about to leave the room I saw a piece of paper on the floor and thought, *If I don't pick that up, someone else will have to.* So I bent down to pick it up, and dunked my tie three inches into the toilet bowl.

Why is lemon juice made with artificial flavor, and dish washing liquid made with real lemons?

5. *Mistaken Identity*

A pastor in Southern California was asked to visit a woman named Margaret in the hospital. Although she was able to speak with him, she was gravely ill. Therefore it was no surprise to him to have someone call a few days later and say, "Margaret died today. Could you take the funeral?"

At the service, the pastor spoke kindly of the woman, giving a little background about her moving from the East Coast to live in California many years ago. This was something he did regularly at funerals. It was an "added touch"—a special gifting he had to comfort relatives by reviving warm memories of the person who had died.

During this time, he noticed that some of the family members were whispering to each other. As he ended his comforting sermon, he casually walked over to the casket and, to his horror, saw that *it wasn't the woman he had visited in hospital!* It was *another* Margaret who had died.

As the relatives quietly filed out the door, he shook their hands and gently whispered, "I'm sorry," to each one.

6.   *Hot Car*

In the late seventies, I ran a Drug Prevention Center which was located on High Street, which is an unfortunate choice of street names for such a place.

One day, I answered the telephone to hear that a member of our drug team had failed to show up at a school to give a talk.

I said that I would get there as soon as possible, and do it myself. Someone in the center threw her keys at me and said, "Take my car. It's a Volkswagen on the third floor of the parking building." I caught the keys, ran up to the third floor, jumped in the car and drove to the school. An hour later, I returned to the building, parked the car and went back to the center.

As I walked in, I threw the keys back and casually said, "What are you doing with a Radio Avon sticker on your car? That's a secular station." She looked curiously at me and said, *"I don't have a Radio Avon sticker on my car!"*

We both ran back to the third floor of the parking building. Sure enough, the keys had fit, and I had taken someone else's car and driven around town for an hour!

Why do we drive on parkways and park on driveways?

7.

Dumb Mutt

It was sometime in the early hours of the morning in July 1995. We had bought a new home and the move had been an opportunity to break our new puppy of the habit of sleeping in our bed. However, in

the blackness of the night I could see the dumb dog lying on the pillow next to me. I had just woken from a deep sleep, and a thousand thoughts raced through my drowsy mind as to why this pup would be back in bed with us.

I reached out my hand and stroked the animal, but felt confused. Its fur seemed a little strange. As I extended my hand to touch it again, to my horror *it began to levitate!* In the eerie darkness, I could see the animal's entire body actually lifting itself up off the pillow and into the air.

I regained my composure, apologized to my wife, Sue, for stroking her hair during the night, and went back to sleep, feeling rather stupid.

8. *Cracking Smirks*

I was running through the New York airport with a very important package in my hand. By the weight of it, it was obviously something of value so the owner would no doubt be *very* pleased when I presented it to him.

About two minutes earlier, I'd noticed the package sticking out from under the seat of a passenger sitting across the aisle from me on the plane. He had obviously forgotten it, and I was the good Samaritan who was taking it to him ... I was *running* the extra mile.

After weaving through a mass of human bodies I spun around a corner and saw the man talking with his friends. What a break, to find him among the crowds. *Was he going to be pleased with me!*

I boldly interrupted his conversation, held the package out and said, "You left this on the plane." He looked puzzled and said that it wasn't his. It was then that someone remarked, "Oh, that's the rolled up emergency equipment—the life jacket, whistle, etc. It must have fallen from underneath the seat."

I could see smirks begin to crack onto a few faces so I backed up and said, "Well ... it was good to see you again. *Bye!*" I felt like the good Samaritan suddenly finding out that the man upon whom he was pouring oil and wine was actually sunbathing.

I made my way back to the plane and with an official air, casually tossed the thing onto the first seat in the plane and walked out.

It was eighteen months before I even told a soul what had happened.

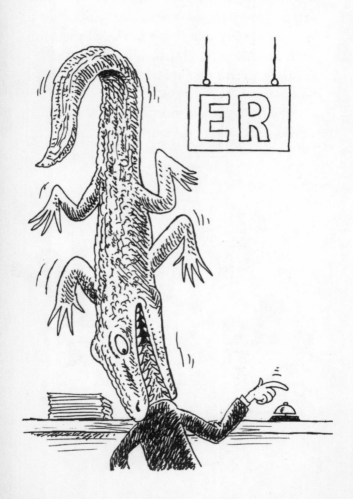

9. *Feeling Down in the Mouth*

About 200 people looked on as alligator wrestler Kenny Cypress of Florida had his head trapped inside a 10-foot, 350-pound alligator for about two minutes. The alligator decided to clamp down on him when beads of his sweat rolled off his face into the alligator's mouth. Friends wedged metal pipes in the alligator's mouth to free the man, who was then taken to Columbia Kendall Medical Center and released a few hours later with holes in his skull and face.

Cypress, who had been putting his head inside alligators for two weeks said, "As long as you don't bump anything in there, you're okay. As soon as something touches the inside, you're in trouble. There's no way to keep the mouth from closing."

Did you hear about the guy whose whole left side was cut off? He's all right now.

10.

Door Number 1

I spoke in a church one Sunday morning, then spent the afternoon with a couple whose church I was to speak at that night. After a relaxing time in their living room, just before we left for the meeting I decided I would use their bathroom. I walked across the living room to the door, and casually opened it to find the man's wife standing at the end of the bed *in her underwear!*

There was a scream like you've never heard, then I pulled myself together, stopped screaming, apologized and closed the door. Unfortunately for me, the bathroom and bedroom doors were identical and side-by-side, and I had opened the wrong one.

11.

Horrors!

One well-known preacher finished his sermon and went down to mingle with his listeners. The man had of gift of making people feel relaxed. He approached a woman in the front row who had a blanket across her, covering what was obviously a small child. As he leaned down, he pulled back the blanket and warmly said, "My... what have we here?" *She was breast-feeding.*

12.

The Dumb Club

I went "door knocking" to let my neighbors know they were welcome at the local church. I was embarrassed that cults had imposed upon many a person's privacy, so when a woman opened a door I said in a sincere and friendly voice, "Hello, I'm not a Jehovah's Witness." She said, *"Well, I am!"*

> *The short fortune teller who escaped from prison was a small medium at large.*

13.

Big Mouth

I was in New Zealand waiting to be picked up by a man to be driven to a meeting. The friend I was staying with said, "The first thing you will notice about Chuck is his big nose." His wife chided him for such talk, but he insisted, "I'm serious. The poor man's nose is *huge.*" I said, "Thanks a lot. Now the first thing I will see is his nose, and I don't want to embarrass the man, so let's not talk about that subject anymore."

That didn't quiet down my twisted buddy. He must have mentioned that man's nose another three or four times. Of course, knowing his twisted sense of humor, I took what he was saying with a large grain of salt. As we were waiting outside for Chuck, I was a little concerned about whether he would have room in his car for my eight boxes of books and tapes.

When he was late, my warped companion said, "I don't know what could have happened to him—he *nose* where to come."

I ignored him. I wanted to be a kind, loving, caring, and warm person, and would rather die than make fun of another person's physical appearance.

Suddenly, Chuck drove around the corner in a *very small* car. As we were introduced, (for some reason) I couldn't help noticing his nose. It was generous, but my friend had been exaggerating. The last thing in the world I wanted to do was to draw attention to it, so I looked at my eight boxes and casually said, "*I hope you have a big* trunk!" As my friend and I stuck our heads into the trunk to arrange the boxes, he choked out, *"How could you say such a thing!"* (Down Under, a car trunk is called the "boot," so unless a New Zealander is famil-iar with the Amercian language, it means an elephant's nose.)

He's probably telling someone right now about the size of my big mouth.

14. *What's in a Name?*

I did a radio interview by phone in September 1995, which I suspect was the first interview the show host had done. It went something like this: "We have a great author on the line today. His name is...ah...ah... Ray Comfort, and his book is *Everyday Evangelism*.[1] Reverend Crawford, how are you doing today? Sorry...Ray Crumfort."

He then got the name correct for a short time but continued: "Tell me this, Evangelist Crawford...ah...Comfort...if you have just tuned in, we are listening to Evangelist Ray Crawford. Tell me, Evangelist Crawford, how do you approach someone with the gospel?...Evangelist Crawford, it was nice to have you with us today."

> *Why do they call it a TV set when you only get one?*

---

[1] Now titled *How to Win Souls and Influence People* (Bridge-Logos Publishers).

15.

Spilled Milk

In Benton, Arkansas, two men were crying
over spilled milk when they broke out of
the county jail and stole a milk truck as a
getaway vehicle. However, the back door of
the truck had been left open and cartons of
milk spewed onto the road behind them,
leaving a milk trail for the local sheriff to
follow. They were apprehended about thirty
miles from the jail.

16.

Feeling Blue

A family in San Diego was in the process of
moving, but because the husband was out
of town, the wife had the unenviable task
of packing the entire household into cardboard boxes. That night, she collapsed with
her young family into sleeping bags on the
floor of their home.

During the night, the weary woman
was roused by her youngest son saying that

there was a bug in the room. She told him to swat it. When he refused, she made her way into the darkness of the garage, grabbed a can of bug spray and, without disturbing the other sleeping children by turning on the lights, sprayed the window ledges and around the sleeping bags of the kids and went back to sleep.

In the morning she found that it wasn't bug spray she had used, but blue spray paint.

> *The guy who fell onto an upholstery machine is now fully recovered.*

17. *Judge for Yourself*

In Rolling Meadows, Illinois, a Cook County correctional officer named Michael Moreci was put under investigation and faced a fine of up to $500 for yelling at a motorist, *"I beat up guys like you for a living!"* The motorist he yelled at was Judge Sam Amirante.

18. *It's Called "Dope" for a Reason*

The year was 1978. I had published a book on drug abuse which had received national publicity. I had also opened a drug prevention center on High Street (a poor choice of street names for a drug center). So it was no surprise when I was suddenly heralded as an expert, and found myself on panels explaining the dangers of drug abuse.

On one occasion I was on a panel with a well-known doctor and the local drug squad in front of around six hundred locals. After the experts had spoken and answered questions, the meeting came to an end.

That's when one concerned mother approached me with her two young boys. Unbeknown to me, at the conclusion of the meeting, the drug squad lit a marijuana joint, so that parents could become familiar with the smell of pot, and it was being passed around so that the smell would be widespread. As I answered the dear lady's questions, her two boys looked on admiringly. I guess I was their hero—fighting the evils of illicit drug use.

As I talked to her, someone tapped me on the shoulder and handed me the still lit joint. I was so caught up in the conversation I hardly gave any thought to what was being passed to me. I simply took the joint in my hand, and while I was still talking . . . took one quick puff and passed it on.

19.   *Dumb Crooks*

In Pensacola, Florida, a man police have dubbed "Bad Luck Brown" held up a store with his finger hidden under his shirt to look like a gun. He made off with the money, but left behind the holdup note written on an envelope with his name and address on it. Then there was the criminal who mugged a cab driver and left his own wallet in the cab.

In East Tennessee, a man walked into a store and realized that he had forgotten his holdup mask, so he put a cardboard box over his head and took off with the money. A week later, he returned to the same store to rob it once again. However, the same clerk was on duty, saw him coming, locked the store and called the police. The man was arrested some time later.

Then there was the brilliant inmate who broke out of prison a day before he was due for release. He was caught and given two extra years.

20. *No Money*

A robber burst into a fast food restaurant
in Portland, Connecticut, before daybreak
and demanded money. However, just as the
restaurant worker was opening the cash
drawer, one of the microwave oven timers
went off. The nervous gunman thought it
was a security alarm and ran out without
getting any money.

21.

Bird Brain

My youngest son, Daniel, called, "Dad, come quick! There's a bird in here!" I love birds, so I quickly ran to see what was going on. Sitting on the carpet was the cutest little bird you could imagine. Often when birds are sick, they will pull their legs into their little bodies and fluff out their feathers. This little fellow had done just that.

Also when birds are sick, they lose their sense of fear of human beings. This one had done just that. He simply sat there with his eyes closed. It was so cute. I knelt on the floor and got right up to his precious little face and said, "Hi there, little fellow..."

Daniel, not knowing as much as I do about the bird world and how the creatures look when they are unwell, said in his simplistic naiveté, "It could be dead." I ignored his unenlightened comment. Sometimes teenagers are better just to keep their silly thoughts to themselves.

I reached out my experienced hand and gently touched the bird. The cute little fellow just rolled over to one side and stuck his cute, stiff little legs in the air. It was deader than a Kentucky fried chicken.

22.   *Bad Taste*

In San Diego in the late 1990s, a man named Tony visited a convalescent home and began speaking with an elderly lady. As he talked, he helped himself to some peanuts from a jar at the side of the old woman's chair.

After some time, he asked the woman if she would like a peanut. She replied, "Oh,

I can't eat the things, dear. I just suck the chocolate off and drop them in a jar beside my chair."

Have you ever imagined a world without hypothetical situations?

23.

Thumbs Up

Bill Brugman is an experienced carpenter.
One Monday afternoon in April 1998, he
hit his thumb with his hammer. It was a
full strength, "right on the nose," bulls-eye
hit. It was so painful, he wept. He then left
his workplace, went home and wrapped his
thumb in ice. He also put his throbbing
digit in a finger-splint and took painkillers.
That night he felt every heartbeat in his
thumb.

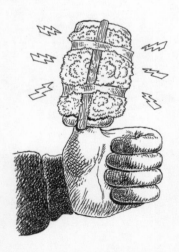

Finally, after a painful and restless night, he dropped off to sleep and awoke in the morning to find that his thumb had finally stopped throbbing. It was much better, so he didn't bother to put the finger-splint back on. Instead, he went outside to get the morning paper, and slammed his thumb in the door.

24. *Blowing it*

Man has a talent when it comes to blowing it. Take for example the experience of an Englishman named Peter Rolands. When he found himself in such cold weather that he couldn't get his key into the frozen lock of his vehicle, he decided to use some ingenuity by blowing warm air into the lock. Unfortunately, his lips touched the freezing metal and locked to it.

As he knelt beside the door of his car, with his lips held fast on the lock, an elderly woman stopped and inquired about whether Mr. Rolands was okay. The poor man responded, "Alra? Itmmlgptk!!!" *at* which the woman became frightened and ran away.

He was trapped in that posture for twenty minutes, until continual hot breathing loosed his chilled lips.

25. *Kind Wife*

I wonder if the man who thought of the bumper sticker "Sometimes I wake up grumpy; other times I let her sleep" had a good relationship with his spouse.

I have a great relationship with Sue. In fact, when I travel I often call her four or five times a day, sometimes for no other reason than to let her know how much I love her.

At first I don't say a word. I just make kissing sounds. I usually get the right number.

One evening as we sat like a pair of doves on our love seat, I decided to gently lean across and lovingly lay my head on her shoulder. That sort of thing is important to a woman.

I lifted the TV remote to put it to one side and accidentally bumped her knee. Her knee was bent and I managed to hit her with the corner of the device, striking a raw nerve that sent pain through her whole body.

I felt terrible. I apologized, then placed the remote on the sofa. Unfortunately, as I did so my watch scratched her leg.

Often on warm evenings I will ask Sue if she would like to go for a romantic walk around the block (that sort of thing is important to a woman). If she is interested, I tell her to return quietly because I will probably be snoozing on the sofa.

The raw nerve incident reminded me of the time I decided to go with her for a romantic walk. As we were strolling together, a woman walked by with a small dog on a long leash. She went to the right and the dog went to the left, so I jumped over the leash. Unfortunately, my back foot kicked Sue in the shin as I jumped. She did a little public dance (she's very talented), then looked down in horror at her leg. A lump the size of an egg, the color of a prune, and the heat of a jalapeno pepper had immediately arisen where I kicked her.

She didn't even get mad at me (she's used to pain). Besides, she loves me, and love covers a multitude of shins.

The first time I tried to kiss her, the seat she was sitting in broke.

She is a very understanding wife. When I have to go out of town for ministry, she often offers to take me to the airport a day early—that's how kind she is.

26. *Note Worthy*

In Baltimore, two men approached a Harbor Bank teller with a note saying, "I have a gun, give me your money or else!"

When the teller read the note (which was written on the back of a deposit slip from *another* bank), she told them, "This is a First National transaction—you'll have to go to First National."

The two crooks looked at each other, panicked, and ran off.

> *Police were called to a day care where a three-year-old was resisting a rest.*

27. *Worn Out*

When our eldest boy was seven years old, his grandmother bought him a uniform of his favorite football team. We thought he looked so good attired in the soft material

that we proudly sent him to school wearing
it the next day.

He quickly returned home the same
morning rather upset. The other kids at
school pointed out that they were pajamas.

28. *The Great Sahara*

I was in Santa Monica, California, filming for our television program, when a young man approached me and said he appreciated our ministry. Then he introduced me to his lovely wife, a solid lady with a pretty face, whose name was Sahara.

I meet thousands of people and have learned the art of making them feel relaxed by simply asking them questions about themselves. This one was a no-brainer. Her name was unusual. Sahara. I'm not only artful in making people feel relaxed, but I'm also well-educated. I knew that the Sahara is the biggest and the most searing sand desert in the world.

So I smiled congenially and revealed my amazing knowledge by saying, "I'm pleased to meet you. 'Sahara'—like the desert?" When she said, "Yes," I asked, "What does the name mean—big and hot?"

As I said the words, somehow they didn't sound right. There is now something bigger than the Sahara. My mouth.

29. **The Tired Lady**

A woman was resting at Venice Beach in
California in the summer of 1994. The
police beach patrol vehicle didn't see her,
and ran over her as she lay face down in

the sand, about fifty feet from the water's edge. The woman, who was deeply impressed with the vehicle they were driving, was treated at a local hospital and discharged the same day.

> *You know that little indestructible black box that is used on airplanes— why can't they make the whole plane out of that same substance?*

30. *Still Squeamish*

Some time ago, some Boeing employees in Washington decided to steal a life raft from one of the 747s. They were successful in getting it out of the plant and home. When they took it for a float on the Stilliguamish River, they were quite surprised by a Coast Guard helicopter homing in on the emergency locator that is activated when the raft is inflated.

31. *Not So Smart*

John D. Smart of St. Louis, Missouri, sustained two broken legs after smashing the window of a stereo shop, using a manhole cover from the sidewalk in front of the store. As he backed away from the window to admire his handiwork, Smart fell down the manhole. I wonder what the "D" in his name stands for?

32. *Fired Fence Builder*

A woman in California hired someone to build a fence in her yard. The fence builder attended her church, but unbeknown to her, he had a secret smoking problem.

After he had been working on the fence for some time, she suddenly drove around the corner and up the driveway of her home to find the man dancing around in a frenzy. He had been having a quick smoke, but when he saw her car pull up the driveway, in a panic he spat the cigarette out of his mouth. It had fallen inside his T-shirt.

33. *Let the Chips Fall*

In 1988 in Flagstaff, Arizona, a woman in her twenties sat with friends around a table in a Mexican restaurant, waiting for food. As usual, the restaurant had served up a large bowl of tortilla chips as an appetizer.

While she chatted with friends, she saw

a chip sitting on the table next to the bowl. Not wanting to be wasteful and knowing that it was a clean table, she picked up the chip and put it in her mouth.

To her surprise, it wasn't crisp, but soft, and it had a peppermint taste. After she removed it from her mouth, she found that when the chips were served, the lady next to her had taken bubble gum from her mouth, squeezed it between two chips and stuffed it close to the bowl.

34. *Pocket Change*

Sue and I have our own chicken coop. I love chickens because I love eggs. I even named each of the birds. There's Fingerlick'n, Tender, Roast, Original, and Crispy. If they don't lay, I point to their names on the coop wall. One day they pumped out five eggs. I could hold only four—two in

each hand—so I very carefully tucked one
in the top of the front pocket of my jeans,
grabbed the other four and went inside.
Five eggs. That's pretty good. Free range,
organic, natural eggs. I couldn't wait to tell
Sue. Five. I was proud of my ladies.

I put the prizes on the kitchen counter
and looked at them. But I'm not stupid; I
knew that something wasn't right. I mumbled, "I thought that there were *five* eggs.
There's only f…" As I leaned forward I
heard a strange "cracking" noise.

35. You've Got to Be Kidding

In 1998 I published a book titled *101 Things Husbands Do to Annoy Their Wives*. As a touch of humor I noted on the cover, "Adapted from One Million and One Things Husbands Do to Annoy Their Wives."

Some time later I received an official letter from the Library of Congress in Washington, D.C. In it a woman explained that they delayed issuing the book a catalog number because "it contains some material which has been adapted from another source." This was an apparent reference to the mention of "One Million and One Things..."

I wrote back and explained: "This is a subtle attempt at humor. There is no book called *One Million and One Things Husbands Do to Annoy Their Wives*. Even if there were that many one-liners, think of how many pages it would be. If we had 10 one-liners on each page, *that would mean the book would be 100,000 pages*. The average Bible is only about 1,000 pages.

"I should hope that it is a stretch of the imagination to think that anyone could find one million and one things that husbands do to annoy their wives. I hope this clarifies the matter."

36. *Finger-licking Good*

I took a package of freshly grated cheese out of the refrigerator. I sliced a tomato, grabbed a generous handful of cheese, and tucked them into bread. Then I warmed the sandwich slightly in the microwave, put salt and pepper on it, and sat down to enjoy my lunch.

I was two-thirds of the way through when the phone rang. I reluctantly left the sandwich on a table by my chair.

As I returned to my delicious morsel a few minutes later, my son mumbled, "I wouldn't eat that food if I were you." I took no notice of him. He often sits in my favorite chair, and getting him to move is like trying to move a beached whale. This was just another teenage tendency to deprive me of pleasure.

The rest of the sandwich was on the counter, so as I walked past I scooped it up and stuffed the remainder of it into my mouth. It was still warm and fresh. The cheese, tomato, salt, pepper, and soft bread caressed my taste buds.

Just then Sue stepped into the kitchen and yelled, "Agghhh! Don't eat that—*I put it on the counter because the dog had been licking it!*"

37. *A Word to the Wise*

I live in the Los Angeles area—the land of movie stars, swimming pools, smog, car chases, and bank robberies. When I'm not driving or riding my bike, I run. I tend to run everywhere. I run up stairs, and I leap down stairs. I always have. Not that I like running. I run because I don't like walking; it's too slow. Sue knows this and only once has she told me that I shouldn't run. She was sitting in our van when she saw me running toward the vehicle, and told me as I got in that she thought it wasn't wise to run out of a bank.

When the smog lifts in Los Angeles,
U.C.L.A.

38. *Good Sound Men*

When I speak at a church for the first time, I am well aware that the congregation is making an assessment of the guest speaker. Their first impression is important—if I goof, it can effect their receptivity to what I say.

When I first stepped into a pulpit in a church in Seattle, Washington, early in 1995, the sound system let out a deafening howl that wouldn't stop. This had the effect of making the congregation jump out of their wits and put their hands over their ears. It also sent the sound men into a panic. They rushed up to the pulpit and grabbed a live microphone that had been placed at my feet. Unfortunately the cord was hooked around a large glass of water and it was knocked over right where I was standing.

When the microphone screamed, the panicking sound men turned off *my* microphone, which meant that I had no volume until they figured out what had happened.

During the sermon, the music stand that was holding my Bible slowly sank under its weight, giving the impression I was steadily growing in stature as I spoke.

> *Why is it that when you're driving and looking for an address you turn down the volume on the radio?*

39. *Catastrophic*

In 1978, during a firemen's strike in Britain, the army was called in to carry out the normal duties of the firemen. During this time they received a call from a very upset elderly woman, whose cat was stuck up a tree.

The army immediately responded to the woman's call and valiantly rescued the stranded animal. The dear woman was so thrilled that she invited the whole group of soldiers into her home to celebrate the event with tea and cookies.

After the celebration, fond farewells

were given. Then off went the army, driving over the cat and killing it.

40. *Just a Little Blood*

I decided to get onto our roof and trim the avocado tree next to the house. I knew how dangerous it would be walking on a steep roof, so I tied a rope around my waist and secured it to an overflow pipe that was sticking skyward.

I could have thrown the rope over the house and tied it to the bumper of my car, but I had heard about a man who did that. His wife, not knowing what he had done, drove off in the car and pulled him over the top. No, I would not do that. Carefulness is my middle name. I climbed up a ladder that was leaning against the tree and scrambled onto the roof. As I did so, I scraped my knee on the bark of the tree and drew blood.

For some reason, my youngest son, Daniel, kept watching me as I tied the rope around my waist, then onto the pipe. I had the thought that either he was concerned for my welfare, or he was a sadist. It was the former, otherwise he wouldn't have pointed out that the rope was too long between me and the pipe and that if I did fall, I would end up hanging over the edge of the roof. He was also helpful by shouting, as I was edging my way down the roof, that the long-handled saw I was carrying was caught on the top of the TV antenna, almost snapping it off.

I cut down the branches without smashing anything. I only spilled a little blood and scratched my face. I hadn't fallen into the trap of tying the rope around the bumper of the car, nor did I succumb to the temptation to noose the rope around my neck to keep it from getting in the way while I was sawing. That would have been a stupid thing to do, as it may have messed up my shirt collar.

Later that week, I cut down a branch that loosened an avocado which hit Sue square between the eyes.

> *I wondered why the baseball was getting bigger. Then it hit me.*

41. *Soap Opera*

I once bought a gadget from a magic shop. It looked like a bar of soap, but underneath it was a spring-loaded surprise. When it was picked up by some unsuspecting soul, it exploded. I purchased it for my teenaged nephew who was coming to stay at our house.

I decided to try it on my 18-year old son *before* I sprung it on my nephew. I carefully pulled the spring back, slipped in the tiny gunpowder cap, and put the bar into his bathroom.

I then casually said, "Daniel, go into the bathroom and wash your hands." He stopped what he was doing and walked into the bathroom without a question. I waited with baited breath. Any second there was going to be a loud bang and a

scream. I waited for 30 seconds. Something was wrong, so I walked into the bathroom and picked up the "soap." It had failed to explode. *I should have read the instructions.*

I stepped up to the soap, and as Daniel stood behind me, I carefully turned it over and touched the spring. Suddenly there was a massive bang right in my face. It seemed to echo around the bathroom walls. *It was so loud it made my ears ring.* My son looked at me for a moment with a blank expression.

He then mumbled, "Roadrunner," and stepped out of the bathroom.

42. *A Screw Loose*

When the cassette radio in my daughter's car wasn't working, I quickly offered to fix it. She had hit a bump on the freeway and it stopped playing, so it was simply a matter of reattaching a loose wire.

I opened the car door and skillfully ran my hand under the dashboard, but couldn't feel anything, so I decided that I needed to *see* what I was doing. I'm not stupid—if I blindly poke my fingers around wires, I could be shocked. The trouble was that the area was so confined, the only way I could see under the dashboard was to maneuver myself upside down across the passenger seat, similar to the way a high jumper goes over a bar.

It was a brilliant move. In that position I could see all the way along the underside of the dash. I had turned the motor on so that the cassette would play if I attached the right wire. Intelligent, huh? Problem. *There weren't any wires*—it was all internal. It was then that I decided I had better maneuver myself out, and discovered an interesting thing. An upside-down human body with its head near a car floor, its back on the seat, and its feet sticking out the door can't move at all.

43. *Take Note*

In Pearson, Florida, a potential bank robber passed a note to a clerk behind the counter, telling her that he was robbing the bank. She told him that he wasn't at a bank, but at city hall. She then informed the confused gentleman that the bank he wanted to rob was in the same building, just across the hall. The man then ran out of the building.

44. *Cool Dude*

While I was a guest speaker at a church,
our family was staying in the guest home
next door on a very hot day. In fact, it
became so hot, I decided to turn on the air
conditioning in the house. I found the unit,
switched it on then went back to the family.

Some time later, my parents arrived.
After staying with us awhile, they remarked

how it must have been one of the hottest days on record. *It sure was hot.* I could feel drips of perspiration running down my face, and after awhile couldn't sit still because of the heat. I began to walk around inside the house to try to find a cool spot.

I even went back to the air conditioner to see if I could pump any more air out of the thing. It was then that I saw my little error. I had turned the powerful heating system on by mistake.

A thief fell and broke his leg in wet cement. He became a hardened criminal.

45. *Calling Card*

A criminal recently broke into a warehouse and carried items out of the back door to his getaway vehicle. After the theft had been discovered, police found that the robber had held the back door open with a folded piece of paper. When they unfolded it, they discovered it was a traffic ticket that had been issued to the man that morning, complete with his name, address, and license plate number.

46. *Pass the Salt*

My friend Todd Friel lived in Minnesota for many years. Living there during the winter means cold weather and dry skin, so his new bride recommended that they purchase a water softener for their whole house. Water softeners were expensive and they spent hundreds of dollars to have it professionally installed, but immediately noticed how amazingly soft their clothes were. They also noticed that they needed far less lotion. It was wonderful.

Two months later, Todd's expert home-owning wife, Susan, asked if he had put salt in the water softener. He thought she was joking. But once she educated him about its necessity, he dutifully checked the salt level. All was well.

Weeks went by and they continued to take showers and proclaim that the water was softer than a baby's bottom lip. They loved it. It was worth every penny. Soft clothes. Soft skin. Who could ask for anything more? Todd continued to check the salt levels and Susan continued to marvel that they still didn't need to add salt.

After six months and hundreds of showers and tons of laundry, she called the

water softener company to ask if their low salt use was normal. The repairman arrived and spent less than a minute before emerging from the utility room to announce that he fixed their water softener. The problem? The installer had failed to plug it in.

> *A dentist and a manicurist fought tooth and nail.*

47. *Never Say Die*

While smuggling $150 million worth of heroin through London's Heathrow airport, a British drug smuggler named Paul Dye recorded his transactions on a sophisticated pocket computer. When he was arrested and British customs seized his computer, he said, "That won't do you any good. I've erased *everything*."

The police took the computer to its manufacturer and found that it was made with a memory bank that stored *every* transaction, even when erased. Dye got 28 years.

48. *Not So Cold Turkey*

A man in one of the Northern States shot a turkey, and put the bird and his gun in the trunk of his car for the drive home. Unfortunately, the turkey wasn't quite dead and it kicked its leg, setting off the gun and shooting the man in the leg.

After he was treated at a local hospital, he was charged for killing a turkey two weeks before the hunting season began.

49. *Soviet Psychic*

A psychic healer from the old Soviet Union tried to use his "powers" to stop a freight train. The train's engineer told officials that the psychic, E. Frenkel, stepped onto the tracks with his arms raised, his head lowered and his body braced.

The Russian newspaper *Sovietskaya Rossiya* reported on October 1, 1989, that investigators, looking into his decision to jump in front of a train, found the answer in the briefcase he left by the side of the tracks. Authorities found notes written by Frenkel in which he alleged, "First I stopped a bicycle, cars, and a streetcar. *Now I'm going to stop a train.*"

Frenkel claimed that halting a train would be the supreme test of his abilities. The train *did* stop, but only after it had run over him.

50. How About a Kiss?

After the bride and groom exchanged their marriage vows, the minister said to the newly married couple, "How about a kiss?" This was a prompt for the symbolic lifting of the veil, giving the husband moral access to his bride.

The bewildered bride thought the minister meant that *he* wanted a kiss, and leaned forward and kissed him!

To write with a broken pencil
is pointless.

51. *Never Mind*

One day Sue needed to have an electric calculator on her desk. She was doing something important on her computer and was frustrated because she couldn't find an electrical outlet. My sharp male eye noticed one of those power strips by the wall under the desk. Problem solved. I love it when my wife needs my help. I am here to serve. I grabbed the end of the cord from her hand, said a manly, "You'll be proud of me," and dropped to my knees to crawl under the desk. Unfortunately, as I did so I knelt with all of my weight on her foot causing her to groan in pain.

Never mind. I could still impress her by quickly getting the calculator to work, so I shoved the plug into the power strip. Unfortunately (I seem to use that word a lot), it had a wide head and it pushed onto the red on/off switch on the power strip. That immediately shut down Sue's computer in the middle of her work.

Never mind. I would just jump up

quickly and console her (as I usually do). Unfortunately, I miscalculated and bumped my head on her desk as I got up. I was surprised that she didn't give me any sympathy. Come to think of it, she didn't say anything about it despite the loud noise it made. I guess she's used to it. I am. I cut my finger making a tomato sandwich the same week. Then I sent two splinters up my finger nail. I was amazed at how I managed to do that.

Never mind.

Why did Kamikaze pilots wear helmets?

52.

Slip Up

Years ago, as I chatted with a friend over breakfast at his home one morning, I stroked what I thought was a dog under the table. I looked down and saw that I was actually stroking his slipper! The mystified dog was watching me and sitting about six inches from my hand.

53. *Watch Out*

A middle-aged woman, attending a neighborhood watch meeting, noticed that her stolen television was in her neighbor's living room. *Then she noticed that her neighbor was wearing her stolen dress!*

The light-fingered individual and her husband were arrested on burglary charges.

54.   *Horse Sense*

Bill Brugman is from Southern California. He is a man's man, with a deep, manly voice. That's why it shouldn't be a surprise to know that he loves horses. If he wasn't a city dweller, he would be a cowpoke roaming the dusty plains. In fact, Bill once owned his own horse.

Some years ago he decided to ride his horse in the country. He took the saddle from his truck, and as the horse stood by a wood fence, his manly arms easily lifted the heavy saddle onto the back of his steed. With a sense of cool excitement, he pulled the saddle-straps tight. Then, with the ease that only an experienced horseman can muster, he mounted the animal and with a firm command, told it to move.

It didn't go anywhere. He had strapped it to the fence.

> *A chicken crossing the road:*
> *poultry in motion.*

55.   *Stepping Up*

A woman in Northern California stepped
down the aisle with great pride on her wedding day. Unfortunately, she also stepped
onto the inside of her dress.

Much to her dismay, her next step also
went onto the inside of her wedding dress,
and had the effect of pulling her, slowly
but surely, headlong toward the floor.

56.   *A Pushover*

A friend told me about a customer in a
store who was searching through a rack for
a pair of pants. A pair must have fallen
onto the floor, and while he was bending
over to pick them up, the manager came
by. As he walked past he lifted his foot and
gave the customer a firm shove on the
hindmost part. He had mistakenly pre-
sumed it was a close friend and fellow
worker.

57. *How Men Shop*

For a couple of years I rode a kid's bike to work. It was compact enough to fit into the back of our van if I didn't want to ride home. I didn't care what people thought. I am comfortable with my manliness. Well, I was comfortable until a couple of kids rode out of their driveway as I rode past. Suddenly, us three kids were riding along together. I felt really stupid. That night, Sue encouraged me to get a bigger bike.

The next day I drove three miles to a store, strode in and grabbed one of the first bikes I laid my eyes on. I came. I saw. I bought. Men don't shop like women. They are warriors. They conquer. They are hunters. They aim and shoot. Men know what they want, and they just go out and get it.

Sue was amazed at how quickly I returned with a new bike in hand. I could tell that she was impressed with it as I wheeled it into the ministry. No more kid's bike for me. This was impressive. I chatted about how high I felt on it and how easy it was to ride, as I ripped the cards from the spokes and removed the guarantee. There were all sorts of silly labels and stickers. I don't mess with labels. I'm a man. I knew what I wanted, and I had it in hand. I simply pulled them off and tossed them into the trash. As I did so, my eye caught the wording on one label. "Lady's bike."

I rode it for a day, and felt worse than I did on the kid's bike. When I went to get another one, Sue wouldn't let me go on my own.

> *Why do they sterilize needles that they use for lethal injections?*

58. *A Closed Door*

A family in New Zealand had a blue parakeet that was so tame, it was regularly released from its cage and allowed to sit on the side of plates at meal times.

During dinner one evening, someone entered the house and left the door open.

The cute little bird saw its chance for total
freedom and flew toward the open door. So
did a family member, who slammed it shut.
She stopped half the bird from getting out.

59.

Big Shoes

A middle-aged woman from Southern California was at a country and western style restaurant, which instead of identifying restrooms as "Men" and "Women," had the restroom doors labeled "Steers" and "Heifers."

She said, "I went in and thought to myself, *Boy, that lady sure has got big shoes!*" She had thought she was a steer when she was actually a heifer. A few seconds later, she realized her mistake and stampeded out of the territory.

Why do they lock gas station bathrooms? Are they afraid someone will clean them?

60. *Honking Hubby*

A man had a habit of honking his car horn each day as he came home from work. His loving and faithful wife, upon hearing the honk, would immediately raise the garage door. He would swing around a sharp corner and drive straight into the open garage.

His wife was consistent in her door-opening ministry, until one day she failed to hear the car horn. Her happy, honking husband swung around the sharp corner, up the driveway, through the closed doors, through the back wall and into the vegetable garden.

61. *A Mind of Its Own*

A police officer in Nebraska accidentally left his vehicle running in "drive" after pulling over a truck for inspection. It sat stationary for three minutes until the air conditioner automatically switched off, releasing more power to the motor. It then drove itself forward, right into the back of the truck he was inspecting.

The officer had just installed a video system in his vehicle, which is now used to train officers on what not to do.

> *He had a photographic memory which was never developed.*

62. *Spied a Bite*

A young lady was in a supermarket in Costa Mesa, California, when she struck up a conversation with a rather large woman.

During the discussion, the woman mentioned that she'd received a spider bite that almost killed her. Fortunately, a doctor had given her medication that fought off the infection.

The woman then lifted her pant leg to show the young woman her bite. When the young lady saw the swollen ankle, she gasped in horror. *Then she noticed that the other ankle was the same.*

The bite was on the woman's knee.

63. *Foot in Mouth*

It has rightly been said, "A closed mouth gathers no foot." A preacher lives by his mouth and often dies by the mouth, because his foot-in-mouth is usually public.

I was once speaking to a congregation about the sinful woman who had washed the feet of Jesus with her penitent tears and dried them with her hair, and said, "*. . . and this woman washed Jesus' hair with her feet!*"

64. *Adam's Apple*

I have always gotten along well with children. In fun, I would tell them to look up at something, and then give them a gentle tap under the chin. Kids love that sort of thing. It's something children need—a grownup to relate to them and give them a sense of self-worth.

I did this routine with my pastor's boys. Of course, they laughed and wanted to do it back to me. Kids are *so* cute. It's part of growing up, to imitate an adult...that's how they learn. Little Alex beamed with joy and said, "What's that up there?" I played along with the cute little fellow and looked up. It's a joy having a built-in gift to be able to communicate in a tangible way with youngsters.

I didn't have to wait for long. I smiled as I gazed upward, waiting for the gentle tap of a child's soft little hand. *The kid gave me a swift karate chop to the throat!*

I don't do this anymore.

65. *Good Acting*

A woman was asked to play the part of a vicious arsonist on the popular television program "America's Most Wanted." She was an experienced actress, so she gladly accepted the part.

The day after the program was aired, two New Jersey police officers walked passed the woman. One stopped, came back and said, *"You're the lady who was on 'America's Most Wanted' last night!"* She smiled at the thought of being recognized in public.

The officers arrested her.

66. *Lack of Evidence*

In Duluth, Minnesota, a man named Jack Pettit was arrested and charged with stealing a neighbor's pig. His attorney maintained that he was innocent and filed a motion that the case be dismissed for lack of evidence. The judge agreed and declared the case dismissed. Jack Pettit then thanked the judge and asked, "But do I have to give back the pig?"

67. *Giant Kiwis*

A few years ago, we were awakened around midnight on Halloween by a noise on our

front lawn. As we peered out the window,
Sue recognized a friend (in his forties)
dashing into the darkened distance.

He had left 220 large pumpkins on our
front lawn, with a huge sign saying "For
sale: Giant kiwis." I thought the situation
was humorous, but Sue wasn't smiling at
all. She is practical minded and wanted to
know what we were going to do with 220
pumpkins.

I called our church food ministry in the
morning and asked if they could use the

pumpkins. They picked them up within the hour.

The next day when I went to the food ministry to lead a Bible study, I was introduced as "the man who donated all those pumpkins." I received a hearty round of applause.

A few days later, my practical-joking friend said (with a straight face) that he had heard about the "terrible incident of the pumpkins being dumped on our property." I told him about how I had been honored for the generous gift. Then I said that I would find out who put them on our lawn, because I had prayed that God would make the guilty culprit's mouth turn up at the edges. That made him smile.

68. *Cut It Out!*

After some searching, Sue and I finally found a quality piece of carpet for our bathroom at a reasonable price. I laid the old carpet down and made a pattern on the new carpet. It was simply a matter of putting it on top of the new piece, cutting it out with a very sharp knife, and positioning it in the bathroom. There was nothing to it.

When Sue warned that I could make a mistake because I had the new piece upside down, I shrugged her off as a fussing female. There are some things that are mundane to men, and this was one of them. In fact, I amazed myself at the speed at which I was able to get the job done.

After I had cut the new carpet into shape, I *ran* with it to the bathroom. I felt excited and pleased that the job was so quick and simple—all because I had had the good sense to use the old carpet as a pattern. I should have been a brain surgeon.

As I stood in the bathroom, Sue came to the door to watch me complete the job. This is the part that gives most of the satisfaction. A man needs the respect of a woman, and this is one way to get it—dazzle them with dexterity.

I skillfully turned the carpet around to fit it in place, and felt a (familiar) hot flush. I looked at Sue and firmly said, "Go out." When she protested, I said again, with more resolution, *"Go out now."*

After she backed out with a (familiar) worried look on her face, I closed the door. I dropped the carpet onto the floor and confirmed my fears. *I had cut the curve around the bathtub the wrong way.*

> *If money doesn't grow on trees, then why do banks have branches?*

69. *On the House*

A friend and I were away from our wives in Hungary speaking at a convention. We were staying in a hotel for a few days, so we decided we would go into the bar to share our faith. There had been many fallen preachers around that time, but Jesus was called the friend of tax collectors and sinners, so that's what we would do—befriend sinners.

As we sat at the bar, we decided to break the ice by doing some sleight-of-hand tricks for the bartender. He was thrilled—so thrilled he decided to show us *his* "magic" by making a martini that had three separate layers of colors. Then he slid the alcoholic beverages across the bar toward us and said the drinks were "on the house." We politely told him that we didn't drink alcohol, and firmly pushed them back toward him. When he pushed them back to us, my friend said, "Please . . . we *don't* drink. Give them to someone else."

So that's what he did. Unbeknown to us, the bartender had the two drinks delivered to two attractive young ladies who

were sitting across the room by themselves. He told them the drinks came from the two unaccompanied men sitting at the bar.

Suddenly, to our horror, we had two strange women trying to sit on our knees. For our next trick, we both disappeared from the scene.

70. *The Winner*

In West Virginia, a man won a game of "chicken" with a train. The 22-year-old and a friend were seeing who could stay on the tracks the longest as the train sped toward them. He beat his friend, but was hit by the train and tossed nearly 70 feet. He was taken to a hospital where he was listed in serious condition.

71. *A Long Stretch*

In Illinois, a 23-year-old man named James Dowdy was sentenced to three years

in prison after being arrested while carrying a bag of stolen socks. At the time, he
was on probation for another sock theft,
and has never been accused of stealing
anything but socks.

Since we are on the subject of socks, a
visiting preacher recently took his jacket off
while in the pulpit, and found a sock stuck
to his shirt by static.

72. *Not for Cat Lovers*

I don't hate cats, although I have to admit that I get mad at them when they fight outside our bedroom window at 3:00 a.m. It's not the nicest of sounds. I do have a friend who really dislikes felines. If you asked him if he liked cats, he would probably say that he does, but that he can't eat a whole one. I once met a dentist who said that he's never run across a cat he didn't like.

I once ran over a cat. I was 18 years old, and I was driving home at around 10 o'clock one dark night. Suddenly, there was a black flash in front on my car, and I heard a distinctive and unforgettable *thoomp, thoomp*. I thought, "Horrors! I've just run over a cat!"

I immediately stopped the car and backed up to see if it was okay, and heard *thoomp, thoomp* again. I thought, "Horrors! I've just backed over the cat I just ran over." I then panicked, put my foot on the accelerator and drove off real fast. As I did so, I heard a now familiar *thoomp, thoomp*.

73. *More Bad Taste*

When I arrived at work one day, I saw a message on my desk: "Call Mr. Lyon—*urgent*." So I immediately dialed the number on the note and heard, "Orana Park Zoo, can I help you?" I said, "Yes, I would like to speak to Mr. Lyon, plea..." I had been the brunt of a practical joke. Calling Mr. L. E. Fant at the zoo is a good follow-up.

Sometimes pranks can backfire. I said to an 11-year-old boy (the one who had chopped me in the throat), "Hey, you should smell the bottom of this swimming pool...it's really neat!" About ten seconds later he came smashing through the surface of the water coughing and spluttering.

I once called the same good-natured young man and said, "Hey, I'm trying to get hold of Chuck and Lisa's phone number—do you know what it is?"

He answered, "No, what is it?"

74. *Break a Leg!*

In Italy in August 1995, an opera singer was accidentally stabbed during a mock sword-fight while on-stage. Two weeks later, he was accidentally shot in the foot during a performance. He triumphantly appeared back on-stage two days later on crutches, fell over and broke his other leg.

75. *Send the Money*

A man once answered a newspaper advertisement which read "New Porsche: $50." After joyfully paying for the car, he asked why the woman had sold it at such a ridiculously low price. She said, "My husband ran off with his secretary on a business trip, and he sent me instructions saying, 'Sell the Porsche and send me the money.'"

76. *Too Complex for Comfort*

I was in the city of Dunedin, New Zealand, staying in a small apartment complex. I was there to speak at a mid-week meeting. When I was driven back to the complex after speaking that evening, I was encouraged that the hosts had left their outside light on for me. I opened the front door under the much appreciated light, then locked the three inside locks behind me. I then walked down the hallway and turned into their bathroom. I stood there in amazement. *These people had renovated their entire bathroom in just two hours! Incredible.* Then it hit me. I was in the wrong apartment! As I crept back down the hallway, I could hear voices coming from the living room. I unlocked the three locks and snuck back to the right apartment. The next day my hosts informed their neighbors of my mistake, which they thought was pretty funny.

77. Without Disturbing the Family

A married man in Riverside, California, was awakened one night by the sound of a loud cricket, playing cricket with its back legs somewhere in his house. The man decided that he would try to ignore it. That didn't work, so he then pretended he was outdoors enjoying a good night's camping. That didn't work, so he got out of bed in the middle of the night and began a full-scale search of the house.

He finally found the noisy creature in the air-conditioning unit of his house.

When he found that he couldn't dismantle the unit, he decided he would spray the noisy insect with some bug spray he had in a bottle in his garage. The bottle was nearly empty, so he merely added water and sprayed the contents into the unit.

He crawled back into bed successfully without disturbing his wife, but soon noticed an unpleasant odor in the room. Even his dog was covering its nose. When he went back to the garage and read the directions on the bottle, he found a warning that the contents were extremely toxic—so toxic, in fact, that the person spraying should use a mask. The label warned that it was harmful to animals and that it should never be mixed with water. The household had to be evacuated that night.

78. *Tough Turkey*

The owner of a large food processing company called a firm that provided him with turkeys, and ordered five hundred of the big birds. During the day, he called back to say that he was having a tough day and asked that they please cut the order in half. They did, and the same day delivered five hundred turkeys, cut in half.

> *Why are there Interstate highways in Hawaii?*

79. *Cold Comfort*

I was running toward the back door of our house and fell over, hitting my arm on the corner wall of our house. It hurt. *Really* hurt. I lay on the ground for about ten minutes until the pain had subsided to mere agony.

I then stumbled into the garage where our youngest son was working. He obviously had heard my loud groaning as I lay on the ground, but he showed no sign of concern. He didn't even look up when I hobbled in. As I held my still throbbing arm I said, "Daniel, how come you didn't come out to see if I was okay? I could have fallen and hit my *head* against the wall and gone insane." He kept working and mumbled, "How would we have known?"

He then suggested that he get a video camera and follow me around for a day so that we could put out a video version of this book.

> *Why do people recite at a play and play at a recital?*

80. *The Big Bang*

When a man's vehicle broke down on a highway, a woman pulled alongside him and asked if she could push-start his car

with her car. He accepted her offer, and
explained that his vehicle was an auto-
matic and therefore needed to be pushed at
35 mph before it would start. The woman
nodded, turned her car around and drove
back down the street. She then did a U-turn
and hit the man's car...at 35 mph!

81. *Green with Envy*

When a couple stopped by to see their
friends' new home, they were asked if they
liked the color of the house. The husband

looked at the green hue and said, "Who in his right mind would paint a house *this* color?"

The new owners had just painted it.

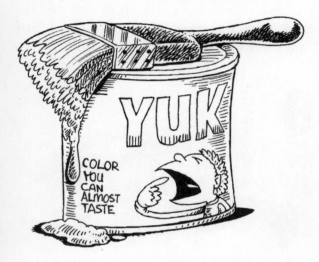

82. *Taking the Time*

In Australia, a man wearing a pair of white coveralls and carrying a ladder walked into a courtroom while it was in session. He climbed the ladder, unhooked the wall clock, and left. He was a thief.

83. *Thoughtful Gift*

Everyone calls my son-in-law by his initials, "E.Z." One reason I like him is that he has a dry sense of humor. When people ask him what his initials stand for, he says, "Elvis Zresley."

He looks lovingly into my daughter's eyes and says, "Open your eyes wide, so that I can gaze into them, and see my reflection." He is also *very* romantic. His gifts to my daughter are *so* thoughtful, I decided I would out-do him on Valentine's Day.

I bought Sue *three* gifts. One was a heart-shaped box of candy. The second was a heart-shaped glass ornament that contained the words "Thank you for being my friend." The third was a mug (not heart-shaped) with these words inscribed on it: "*A worthy woman. Strength and dignity are her clothing and she smiles at the future* (Proverbs 31)." It was so applicable, I didn't even look at it twice when I saw it in a store. I swept it up, gave it to the cashier, and it was put straight into an attractive box.

Sue was thrilled to read the thoughtful (better than son-in-law) wording on its side. However, when she turned it around, I saw another word on the other side of the mug that I hadn't seen before. It said "Mother."

Why do people say they "slept like a baby" when babies wake up every two hours?

84. *After Her Own Kind*

My mom (who takes after me) pulled in behind two cars and waited patiently to turn onto a one-way street. After some time she realized the cars didn't have drivers. They weren't waiting to go around the corner—they were *parked* on the side of the road.

85. *On Their Way Out*

A Munich schoolteacher once said that ten-year-old Albert Einstein would "never amount to much." In 1962, the Decca Recording Company said as they turned down the Beatles, "We don't like their sound. Groups of guitars are on their way out."

86. *Only Once*

Before her wedding, my daughter, for some reason, was worried that I would step on her dress as I walked her down the aisle. *I can't understand why.*

Despite the fact that I was present, the

wedding was perfect. I didn't step on her dress. I didn't blow my "one-liner" when I gave my daughter away. I didn't spill a drink or get food on my chin. I only blew it once. *Just once.*

Moments before the ceremony, I saw an inch-long piece of fluff on one of the brides-maid's dresses. It was sitting on a dark blue dress, about three inches from the young lady's shoulder seam. When I said, "Would you like me to remove that piece of fluff?" she said, "Yes." So, in a gentlemanly fash-ion, I reach out, took hold of it and pulled.

The "fluff" stretched out to about three inches. My good sense told me something was wrong. This "good sense" was aided by the fact that the young lady wriggled strangely, and the fluff refused to budge. *It was a frayed strand of her bra strap!*

87. *Hard to Swallow*

My son-in-law is a perfect match for my daughter. They both walk and talk in their sleep. For the first two weeks of their marriage, they hardly got any sleep, because they kept talking in their sleep and waking each other up.

One night, Rachel couldn't sleep. She was sitting in the living room in the early hours of the morning, when she heard a loud gagging noise coming from the bedroom. Then her husband walked in and said, "I swallowed an elephant nipple-cover!" He was walking in his sleep, and

totally convinced that he had swallowed an "elephant nipple-cover"... if there is such a thing. Rachel found that hard to swallow, so she asked him if he was awake. That's when he became a little upset, and said, *"Of course I'm awake... I just swallowed an elephant nipple-cover!"* Then he mumbled something about her taking him to the emergency room, and stormed off.

Moments later, he said that he had swallowed a towel. (I guess that's what you should swallow if you find you have an elephant nipple-cover stuck in your throat.) They're a perfect match. I introduced them.

88. Hair-raising Experience

A preacher in Long Beach, California, had just finished a sermon on a hot night when a small, elderly woman asked for prayer. As was the custom of the church, he gently laid both of his hands on her head, prayed for her, then lifted his hands. Unfortunately, his sweating hands stuck to the woman's hair spray. The wig she was wearing stuck to his hands and lifted up when he tried to remove them.

> *Why do they put braille dots on the keypad of the drive-up ATM?*

89. *Fired on the Job*

I was making a cup of tea early one morning. As I reached over a gas burner on the stove I suddenly heard a *woof* noise, and looked down to see that the sleeve of my white bathrobe was on fire. Then I heard another *woof* as the fire quickly spread around to the back of the robe, and another little *woof* as it spread to the sleeve on the other side.

It was around that time that I remembered I had purchased a fire extinguisher for such an occasion. What was I supposed to do now? "Stand six feet from the flame and aim the extinguisher at the base." This wasn't going to be easy. I took the robe off and threw it to the floor, and heard another *woof* as the whole thing caught fire. The manufacturers of the item had obviously soaked it in gasoline to make life more exciting for the wearer.

It was then that my daughter walked back into the room and said, "Dad! I can't believe this. I leave the room for two minutes and while I'm away, you manage to catch on fire."

I learned two valuable lessons from the incident. First, don't lean over an open flame in a bathrobe, and second, a man on fire moves rather quickly.

At the risk of seeming like I'm a klutz or something worse, let me tell you about a minor incident that took place when I was cooking dinner for Sue. She is a hard worker and after a long day at the ministry I like her to come home to a stress-free dinner. It was late in the afternoon, so I decided to cook some fish in oil. I had never cooked in oil, so that would be a pleasant change for her.

I carefully placed the frying pan onto the gas stove. I then skillfully poured the oil into the pan, making sure that not a drop went onto the stove. I had noticed that when Sue gets home she will often grab a sponge and wipe the counter or stove (she's a clean freak), and my goal was to keep her stress-free. Not the tiniest drop hit the stove top. Carefulness is my middle name.

I often visualize myself having a "Comfort Food" television program, where I expertly teach people the do's and don'ts of cooking. I turned on the burner, making sure the flame was high, but not too high. I then took a piece of specially prepared fish from the refrigerator and carefully dropped it from about six inches into the half-inch of very hot oil in the pan. *Kahboosh!* would probably be the right word to describe the noise that came the second the fish hit the pan.

(Note to readers: Never "drop" anything into very hot oil because it splashes and tends to explode as it hits. Also, when cooking with oil, it is wise to use about one thirty-second of an inch on the bottom of the pan. Not half an inch. That much oil tends to make a big splash.)

I leaped back in horror and stared at the two-foot-high, ten-inch-wide pillar of flame that roared in front of me. Man, did it roar! Despite this, I didn't panic. Like a trained professional, I quickly grabbed the fire extinguisher and skillfully aimed it at the fire. It was out in about a second and things were back to normal. No problem.

No problem?! The kitchen was filled with white and stinky smoke. The counter, the stove, the sink, the floor... everything looked like it was covered in a blanket of pure white snow. Yikes! Sue would be home in ten minutes! I rushed to the back door and opened it. Then to the front door and opened it. I turned on a huge exhaust fan to get the smoke out of the house. In seconds it had cleared. Now it was just a matter of... a van was pulling up the driveway! It was Sue. She had left a little early, after a hard day at the ministry, to come home to her usual stress-free dinner!

I casually rushed out to the driveway, where, for some reason, she had stopped the van. The window was down and she had a concerned look on her face. She asked, "Why are the doors open? What's going on?" I smiled and said, "Hi, Love, do you want to drive around the block for five or six minutes?" That was about the time I estimated it would take to remove the "snow" from the kitchen. It took two of us about an hour to clean up.

Sue still lets me cook dinner. I will not be doing a television show.

90. *The Wedding Gift*

A professional video photographer in Jacksonville, Florida, was asked to video-tape a wedding. Unfortunately for him, he unwittingly arrived at the wedding with the camera turned on. This meant that when the bride arrived, he unknowingly switched the camera off to film her.

When the important part of the cere-mony was over, he switched the camera on, thinking that he was switching it off. Then he began to bad-mouth to a friend about the bride's weight. Meanwhile, the camera, which he thought was off, was recording his every word.

After the wedding ceremony, he took the video to the bride and groom and gave it to them as a gift. After viewing the video, they gave him a court summons as a gift.

Why is the person who invests your money called a "broker"?

91.

Sandprints

As I stood at the checkout of a well-known hardware chain, a lady gasped and pointed to the floor. There was a pile of white sand pouring from a fifty-pound bag that I had placed in my shopping cart. I had acciden-tally made a hole in it when I lifted it up a few minutes earlier. I looked behind me and saw *a 180-foot trail of white sand going back through the store to where I had begun my journey.* The sand was thin when I had sped up and thick when I had slowed down. Its trail showed when I had turned to the left, and when I had turned to the right.

92. *More Cold Comfort*

My wife is very reserved. When she bought an ice cream at a mall, held it out and said, "Here you are...handsome," my heart skipped a beat. She didn't usually talk like that! I was about to blush when I realized that I had misheard what she said. She actually said, "Here you are... *have some*."

A similar thing happened a few months earlier. I had called her from out of town when she said, "I will see you tomorrow morning...baby." Baby! *Wow!* I was excited, until I asked her to repeat what she had said. She said, "I will see you tomorrow morning... *maybe*."

93. *Give Me a Brake*

In April 1970, a Mrs. Miriam Hargrave set a new world record. As she drove through a series of red lights, she failed her driving test, bringing the total to thirty-nine failed tests. In the preceding eight years, she had received over two hundred driving lessons. Trailing far behind her was a woman from Auburn, California, who failed her driving test in the first second. She got into the car, said, "Good morning" to the tester, started the engine and shot straight through the wall of the Driving Test Center. She mistook the accelerator for the clutch.

94. *Leave it!*

A husband and wife once had the task of driving me to an airport, and as we had an hour to spare, they kindly took me to lunch.

As the gentleman sat close and chatted, I detected a one-inch hair that was stuck on the outside of his glasses. I believe that it's very important to look someone in the eye when they are speaking to you, and this hair was beginning to look like a massive log that was breaking the eye-line. Besides, I'm a bit of a neat-freak. I thought I'd do the nice man a favor.

While he was still chatting, I carefully reached out and took hold of it with my agile fingers to remove it. It did come off his glasses, but there was a little resistance. *This was because it was still attached to his eyebrow!* I didn't feel that I had the liberty

to pull it out by the roots, so I wisely lifted it up, tucked it into bed, gave it a little kindly pat, and we carried on with the conversation as though I hadn't done what I had just done.

The incident was one of life's little lessons. I learned that day that some things are best left alone.

A few years later I felt greatly comforted when my wise son-in-law (who wrote the Foreword for this book, warning you about me) saw a one-inch hair on the shirt-collar of my eldest son's tuxedo. It was his wedding day, so E.Z., being as kind as I am (and an ultra neat-freak), firmly grabbed it with his fingertips to remove it. Jacob protested in pain. It was an attached chest hair.

So if you and I ever meet, and you (bravely) come close to chat, and I notice a deceased long-haired cat stuck to your glasses, trust me, I won't even mention it.

> *If you have a bunch of odds and ends and get rid of all but one of them, what do you call it?*

95.   *Slam Dunk*

My associate, Mark, and I were enjoying dinner with a pastor after I had preached at his church. I was polite and respectful, not wanting to leave this man with the impression that I did dumb things. During the meal, Mark kicked me under the table and pointed to his teeth. I had trained him well. He had often seen me do that same thing to people over a meal, just to bug them. Again I felt a kick under the table and again he pointed to his teeth. He even followed it up with weird facial gestures, so I casually ran my tongue over my front teeth and found a piece of lettuce the size of a circus tent stuck to my front tooth.

A few weeks later I stood to my feet at a dinner table in a restaurant and said farewell to a pastor who had to leave early. His wife was ill and couldn't join us for the meal, so I asked if she would like a copy of *Comfort, the Feeble-minded*,[2] the book about

---

2 The original title of this book.

dumb things I used to do. He said that she would appreciate a good laugh, so I handed him the book, then reached across the table to shake his hand. As I did so, my good silk tie bobbed up and down in my bowl of bean soup.

96. *Hertz Hurts*

A man who took the Hertz Corporation to court is probably regretting his action. He maintained that the car rental company owed him $17.90 as an insurance refund. Instead of calling the company and trying to negotiate a settlement, he took them to court. He lost the case when the jury sided with Hertz. He had $450,000 in legal fees.

97. *A Shocking Sight*

A woman came home to find her husband in the kitchen, shaking frantically, with what looked like a wire running from his waist toward the electric kettle. He was obviously being electrocuted! Thinking quickly, she grabbed a piece of wood sitting by the back door and whacked him with it.

He was actually listing to his Walkman.

If flying is so safe, why do they call the airport the "terminal"?

98. *Bank Robbers and Burglars*

In Houston, Texas, police set out with their sirens wailing to chase three bank robbers who had merged into freeway traffic. Unbeknown to the police, two burglars who had just pulled a job were also on the freeway, and took off at high speed mistakenly thinking that the law was chasing them. The police immediately did give chase... and apprehended the men after they crashed their car in a panic.

99. *On a Wing and a Prayer*

I had been asked to speak at a church called the New Life Center in the town of Halswell, New Zealand. The meeting was due to begin at 7:00 p.m. As I didn't want to be late, I arrived 20 minutes early and sat outside in my car. I could see a group of people gathered in a hall. I waited for a moment to make sure I wasn't going to burst into a Boy Scout meeting or something and make a fool of myself. I could see more people entering the building so I went in myself.

Sure enough, it was a church meeting. People were seated and musicians were tuning up, so I asked them for the location of the prayer meeting. They directed me to a back room, where I quietly entered, sat down and spent some time praying with the local brethren. Then, just before 7:00 p.m., the last "Amen" was said and eyes were opened. *They were all centered on me!* It was very strange, so I asked, "New Life Center?" "Nope. Saint Mark's. New Life

Center is down the street." Wrong prayer meeting. Wrong church. Now I was late.

100. *Trying It for Size*

In Florida, a 24-year-old tree trimmer, employed just seven months, was fifty feet up a tree trimming branches. He was wearing a safety belt attached to a life-line.

Unfortunately, he cut the branch to which he was attached and fell to his death.

Harold Lee Duncan was mowing his lawn under the watchful eye of his dear wife and his two children. Suddenly, he grabbed his left side, staggered a few steps, collapsed, and died. A small piece of wire, about half an inch long and no wider than a pencil lead, had been hurled into his heart by the lawnmower he was using.

Mario Cianca entered a funeral parlor and saw a man suddenly sit up in a coffin and smile. Cianca was so shocked by the sight, he collapsed and died of heart failure. The owner of the parlor, Pedro Fernandez had been in the coffin, trying it for size for a client who was approximately his height.

Carlos Umbros was fishing in Pampanga in the Philippines. According to a police report, when he opened his mouth to yawn, a fish jumped in and became lodged in his throat. The man choked to death before the fish could be removed.

Why are there flotation devices under plane seats instead of parachutes?

101. *Dumb Crooks*

On October 6, 1998, two men burst into the Foothill Bank in Rowland Heights, California, and robbed it. Unfortunately for them, a witness called the police and a car chase ensued for the next two hours. This was broadcast live over television during which time it was revealed how much the robbers got away with—a cool $486. Despite the pathetic take, they were charged with armed robbery and felony invasion.

During the chase the commentator said what all commentators seem to say during live car chases: "Why don't these guys just give up? They can't get away. Nobody ever gets away. The helicopter will track them wherever they try to hide. If the helicopter loses sight of them, the law will bring in police dogs. They can't get away—why don't they just give up?"

The incident reminded me of why I am a Christian. For years I ran from the Law— not the law of man, but the Law of God. In God's sight, I was a felon. This is what the

Law said: 1) Is God first in your life? Do you love Him with all of your heart, soul, mind, and strength? Do you love your neighbor as yourself? Does your love for your family seem like hatred compared to the love you have for the One who gave those loved ones to you? 2) Have you made a god in your own image, to suit yourself? 3) Have you ever used God's holy name in vain, substituting it for a four-lettered filth word to express disgust? 4) Have you kept the Sabbath holy? 5) Have you always honored your parents implicitly? 6) Have you hated anyone? Then the Bible says you are a murderer. 7) Have you had sex before marriage? Then you are a fornicator and cannot enter Heaven. Have you lusted after another person? The Bible warns that you have committed adultery in your heart. 8) Have you ever stolen something (irrespective of its value)? Then you are a thief. 9) If you have told just one lie (even if you call it "white"), you are a liar, and cannot enter the Kingdom of God. Finally, have you ever desired something that belonged to someone else? Then you have broken the Tenth Commandment that says, "You shall not covet."

Who hasn't broken that Law? We are all guilty, and we are all running. *Why don't we just give up?* We can't get away. Every time we sin, the Bible says that we are storing up wrath that will be revealed on Judgment Day. Every sin we commit is seen by the omniscient eye of a holy God. He has given us a conscience that will eventually sniff us out—we can't get away. Besides, our "take" isn't worth the punishment. God doesn't want to give us justice. He is not willing that any go to Hell, and He has made a way for us to be saved from His wrath.

The Bible says, "God demonstrates His own love toward us, in that while we were still sinners, Christ died for us." He gave His

LAWBREAKERS

sinless life on the cross, showing the depth of God's love for us. We broke God's Law, and He paid the fine so that we could be free from its perfect demands. Then He rose from the dead, defeating the power of the grave. If you repent, trust in the Savior, and obey His Word, God will forgive your sins and grant you everlasting life. The Bible says that all humanity is held captive to the fear of, and power of death (Hebrews 2:15). If we don't face our fear of death, we will run from it until the day we die—and that day *will* come, often unexpectedly. The proof of our sin will be our death. Today, not only face the reality that you will die, *but do something about it ... please*. Obey the gospel and live. Confess your sins to God, put your faith in Jesus Christ, then read the Bible daily and obey what you read. God will *never* let you down.

Thank you for taking the time to read this book. Please feel free to write to me or visit our website:

Living Waters Publications,
P.O. Box 1172, Bellflower, CA 90706, USA
(800) 437-1893; www.livingwaters.com

World's Funniest One Liners

- Ninety-nine percent of lawyers give the rest a bad name.
- Borrow money from a pessimist—they don't expect it back.
- Time is what keeps things from happening all at once.
- Lottery: A tax on people who are bad at math.
- I don't suffer from insanity; I enjoy every minute of it.
- Always go to other people's funerals, or they won't go to yours.
- Few women admit their age; few men act it.
- If we aren't supposed to eat animals, why are they made with meat?
- Give me ambiguity or give me something else.
- We have enough youth. How about a fountain of "Smart"?
- He who laughs last thinks slowest.
- Campers: Nature's way of feeding mosquitoes.
- Always remember that you are unique—just like everyone else.
- Nuke the Whales.

- Consciousness: That annoying time between naps.
- There are three kinds of people: Those who can count and those who can't.
- Why is "abbreviation" such a long word?
- I started out with nothing and I still have most of it.
- Change is inevitable, except from a vending machine.
- Out of my mind. Back in five minutes.
- Laugh alone and the world thinks you're an idiot.
- Sometimes I wake up grumpy; other times I let her sleep.
- The severity of the itch is inversely proportional to the ability to reach it.
- You can't have everything; where would you put it?
- Okay, who stopped the payment on my reality check?
- We are born naked, wet and hungry. Then things get worse.
- 42.7 percent of all statistics are made up on the spot.
- Be nice to your kids. They'll choose your nursing home.
- Humpty Dumpty was pushed.

- If at first you don't succeed, destroy all evidence that you tried.
- I wonder how much deeper the ocean would be without sponges.
- I took an IQ test and the results were negative.
- Nothing is fool-proof to a sufficiently talented fool.
- On the other hand, you have different fingers.
- I've only been wrong once, and that's when I thought I was wrong.
- I don't find it hard to meet expenses. They're everywhere.
- I just let my mind wander, and it didn't come back.
- Don't steal. The government hates competition.
- All generalizations are false.
- The more people I meet, the more I like my dog.
- Work is for people who don't know how to fish.
- For every action there is an equal and opposite criticism.
- IRS: We've got what it takes to take what you've got.

- I'm out of bed and dressed. What more do you want?
- I used to think I was indecisive, but now I'm not too sure.
- If everything is coming your way, then you're in the wrong lane.
- Gravity always gets me down.
- This statement is false.
- Eschew obfuscation.
- They told me I was gullible...and I believed them.
- According to my best recollection, I don't remember.
- It's bad luck to be superstitious.
- The word "gullible" isn't in the dictionary.
- Honk if you like peace and quiet.
- Despite the cost of living, have you noticed how it remains so popular?
- Save the whales. Collect the whole set.
- The early bird gets the worm, but the second mouse gets the cheese.
- Corduroy pillows: They're making headlines!
- Nobody's perfect. I'm a nobody.
- Ask me about my vow of silence.
- The hardness of butter is directly proportional to the softness of the bread.

- Diplomacy is the art of letting someone else get your way.
- If ignorance is bliss, then tourists are in a constant state of euphoria.
- If at first you don't succeed, don't try sky-diving.
- I can handle pain until it hurts.
- If Barbie is so popular, why do you have to buy her friends?
- Stop repeat offenders. Don't re-elect them!
- I intend to live forever. So far so good.
- Who is "General Failure" and why is he reading my hard disk?
- What happens if you get scared half to death twice?
- I used to have an open mind but my brains kept falling out.
- Energizer Bunny arrested; charged with battery.
- I didn't use to finish sentences, but now I
- I've had amnesia as long as I can remember.
- Bills travel through the mail at twice the speed of checks.
- What's another word for "thesaurus"?
- I went to the fights, and a hockey game broke out.